A FEW THINGS I LEARNED ALONG THE WAY

CHRISTA FLACK

ISBN 978-1-68570-471-1 (paperback)
ISBN 978-1-68570-472-8 (digital)

Copyright © 2023 by CHRISTA FLACK

All rights reserved. No part of this publication may be reproduced, distributed, or transmitted in any form or by any means, including photocopying, recording, or other electronic or mechanical methods without the prior written permission of the publisher. For permission requests, solicit the publisher via the address below.

Christian Faith Publishing
832 Park Avenue
Meadville, PA 16335
www.christianfaithpublishing.com

Printed in the United States of America

CONTENTS

To the Newly Beloved in Christ 1
To My Frontline Friends 3
Vile Praise 5
You Never Know 7
Smile 9
Issues 11
Be Careful What You *Don't* Teach Your Children! 12
Oh! The Beauty of It All 14
On Purpose 16
Bitter Cup 18
Stand on It 20
Brace 22
You Have Need of a *Re-* 24
Can I Get a "Wow!"? 28
Growing Together in Christ 30
Silent Night 32

To the Newly Beloved in Christ

I HAVE WRITTEN THIS BOOK because I believe you were created for greatness. God has put so much in you that it can already be seen. Don't lose that, and don't take it for granted. You are smart, you are gifted, and you are blessed. Don't ever let anyone tell you otherwise. With that in mind, here are a few things I learned along the way.

1. Your relationship with Jesus Christ is the most important relationship you will ever have. Choose him first, and he will guide you in all your other relationships and set your priorities. You are human, so know you will still make mistakes, but you can always get back on track. Learn from your mistakes, ask forgiveness, and let him take control.
2. Study your passion. If you have a relationship with Christ, your passion will include your God-given gifts, and your gifts will make room for you. No matter what your passion, study to be the best you can be, and God will do the rest.
3. Don't just live. Thrive! Be curious. Do what you can and know to do. Then push yourself to learn more. You will be surprised at how much you don't know. Always be excited and ready to learn new things.
4. Learn the difference between joy and happiness. Then choose joy. Happiness is powered by emotions and exterior influence that ride on a roller coaster. It can disappear at the mountain top or around a sharp curve, but joy…joy is like a slow, steady train that is powered by God's love and

peace. It stays on an even track through sunshine, storms, and even dark tunnels.

5. Obedience to God truly is better than sacrifice. The sacrifices you make may end up lasting you a lifetime…or ending your life. In a moment of now, you may end up sacrificing your health, your freedom, your finances, your relationships, or your character. Outside of God's love, respect is hard enough to earn and even harder to regain.

I pray that I have sparked a desire in you to press into your relationship with God. He has begun such a great work in you. He will complete it. Enjoy the journey and thrive!

Your sister in Christ,
Christa Flack

To My Frontline Friends

I FEEL LED TO LET you know that I appreciate you. I am not able to be by your side. I only have in my toolbox prayer and words of encouragement. So here it goes…

> Heavenly Father,
> Please show your grace and mercy to all those who are standing in the gap during this time. Shield them with your angels. Keep them safe through this day and the days to come. Allow them to count their blessings in the midst of horror. Show them they do make a difference, that their work is not in vain. Place this thank you in their hearts. Show them your love and give them peace. Take care of their hearts' desires as they take care of others. Bless them as only you can. Amen.

To the medical teams, including nurses, doctors, EMTs, technicians of any kind, custodians, staff members, cooks, and clerks, thank you.

To the farmers, food producers, delivery truck drivers, stockers, cashiers, and greeters, thank you.

To the police departments, fire departments, 911 operators, construction workers, plumbers, electricians, and HVAC technicians, thank you.

To restaurants that are feeding the needy, the volunteers who are reaching out to the homeless, and the people coming up with new and better ways to do things, thank you.

To the seamstresses making masks just to give them away, thank you.

To people movers, cargo movers, and animal caretakers, thank you.

To the churches that stream online, newscasters who speak the truth, and platforms that keep us entertained, thank you.

Not everyone gets to see tomorrow, but for those around today, thank you. Thank you. Thank you for fighting for one more day. Thank you for keeping your promise to hold on, to be strong, to stay okay as best you can. Thank you for being. Thank you. Thank you. Thank you.

From a grateful me

Vile Praise

And David danced before the Lord with all *his* might;
and David *was* girded with a linen ephod.

—2 Samuel 6:14 KJV (emphasis added)

WHEN I WAS SINGING IN the choir, people used to come to me and tell me how much they loved watching me sing. Notice I said *watching me*, not *hearing me*. Don't get me wrong. I am no Yolanda Adams, but I do all right. They liked to watch me because I was all in. I would close my eyes, lift my head, move my hands, dance a little, cry a little, smile a lot...because I was so grateful to God even for allowing me to sing to him. Most of the time I was in my own little worship service, singing for him and him alone. You see, I have chronic obstructive pulmonary disease, or COPD, by combination of emphysema and asthma. By all rights, my condition should have made it impossible for me to sing...but God!

There is a song by Stephen Hurd entitled "Undignified Praise." The words are "I will dance. I will sing and be crazy for my King. Nothing, Lord, is hindering this passion in my soul. And I'll become even more undignified than this!" I love that song because it expresses how I feel whether I'm singing praise and worship at church, in my home, or even in my car. I can imagine David dancing and singing to that song. In 2 Samuel 6:22 (KJV), David told his wife Michal he would be even more "vile" in his praise to the One who put him in the position he was in. Some modern versions changed the word *vile* to a more pc "undignified" (NIV) or "foolish" (NLT). But why use the word *vile*? Such an evil word. *Vile* is defined as being morally despicable or abhorrent; physically repulsive, degrading, and disgustingly or utterly bad. So why use that word?

I believe it was because that word is raw, it is real, and it is passionate! David showed all of Israel just how indebted to God he was, that he would do anything for God—even embarrass himself before all the people. The problem was Michal did not join him in his praise. She was too dignified for such things. I believe she felt more entitled than grateful that she was the wife of the king, and that was her downfall. God did not punish David for his vile praise. But she bore no children, which, in and of itself, was a curse to women in those times.

I always felt I was singing to an audience of one whether I was singing a solo, a duet, or in a full choir and I was just inviting everyone else to join me in that freedom of praise and worship. I always thought it strange when people would say they loved watching me because I didn't want them to watch me. I was inviting everyone to join me. I feel it is the difference between me demanding my kids to hug their father and me showing it is okay to hug their father. I hug him myself while I reach out an arm to them to invite them in as well.

There is no need to feel embarrassed showing your gratitude to God. David was a man, a king, after God's own heart. And he had no problems showing the world his gratitude to God, for God is the one who deserves all your hugs, your songs, your passion, and your vile and undignified praise.

You Never Know

> Pleasant words are as an honeycomb—sweet
> to the soul and health to the bones.
>
> —Proverbs 16:24 KJV

BACK IN THE DAY, WHEN people used to mail in bill payments, I would send in note cards instead of using the envelope provided by the company. Sometimes I would just write "Hello" or "Thank you." Sometimes I would write a scripture or just say I was praying for them. I've always liked writing letters and cards just to let people know I was thinking of them. When I was volunteering at my church, I would send out mass emails to the women of the church, encouraging them to come out to our monthly events. I've even sent out little cards to my landlords with my rent check. Sounds crazy, huh? I have found that it's not so crazy after all. People have helped me understand that you never know about a kind word.

When the revolution of electronic payments was beginning, I was still mailing in most of my credit card payments. I think it was mostly because I liked sending them cards. Then for some reason, I stopped sending cards. I've prided myself on consistently making my payments on time. But when we got stationed overseas, my credit card bills didn't immediately get forwarded, and I had to contact the companies.

By this time, I'd had my favorite credit card for more than ten years, and I knew my payment was late. I knew there would be a penalty, but I wanted to get it done, so I called the company and was greeted by a nice young lady who was able to help me. I explained to her I had not received my bill yet and would send in my payment immediately but needed to make sure the address they had was current. After I gave her my full name and credit card number and I verified who I was, she said, "Wait." I could hear the excitement in her voice but didn't understand why. She asked if I used to live in California and send cards in with my payments. I told her yes, and she began to tell me how she and others used to look forward to getting those cards and how they missed them. Small world. With people constantly complaining and sending in nasty notes, she said it was nice to get a card that just said "Hello" with a big smiley face drawn or "I pray you're having a great day." Without knowing who she was, I had on occasion made her day brighter. She immediately made a note in my record and canceled the late charge against my account.

When I went back to college, I stopped writing emails to the ladies in our church because I thought I was too busy and was quickly told my letters were missed. No one ever wrote back, so I didn't realize the impact my letters had. When I stopped writing them, I was told how much they encouraged our ladies. Some ladies saved them to read whenever they were having a bad day.

I've heard it often said, you should always treat others nice because you never really know what they are going through. I would add, *even those you may never see.* A kind word can go a long way to brighten someone's day.

Smile

I will praise thee; for I am fearfully *and* wonderfully made: Marvelous are thy works; and *that* my soul knoweth right well.

—Psalm 139:14 KJV (emphasis added)

I WAS IN A WOMEN's meeting, and we were asked what the favorite part of our body was, the part we liked most. Some answered their eyes or their legs, some their hair, and some their hands. I said my smile, and I got the funniest looks. My smile isn't pretty. I sucked my thumb as a child, so my top teeth stick out a bit. My bottom teeth are crowded so that some sit back and others are pushed forward. Due to an accident I had when I was young, I broke my top front teeth. The dentist filed them down so they would look even, but both are dead and discolored. I could use some braces but choose not to put myself through that. Like I said, my smile isn't pretty. So some may not understand why I chose to say my smile.

Most of the ladies answered what they felt was their best-looking feature. My answer was based on not how my smile looks but how the act of smiling makes me feel. When I smile, I feel good. In that moment, I know there is hope, I know there is grace, and I'm in a comfortable situation. I know I am not alone, and I feel good about me. That's what my smile does for me. My legs don't do that for me. Nor do my eyes, my ears, or even my tush. However, I must admit I smile sometimes because I like the way they look.

There was a time in my life when I didn't smile. Actually, I can say there still are times. But there was a time when I didn't feel loved.

I believed it when people said I was ugly and stupid. But God... I started reading God's Word, and I began to understand how much God loved me. I realized I was more than what others thought of me. Like the words to a country song, I can honestly say I had looked "for love in all the wrong places." Well, not all...but quite a few. Looking back now, I realize I was already beautiful, smart, and talented but I was waiting for someone else to tell me I was. Anyone. I was looking for validation. I was always pressing for compliments from any and every one, but God has told me his "grace is sufficient." God made us in his image, and there is nothing ugly or stupid about God. Our value can only be validated by the One who created us. All other opinions are just that, opinions. And I think it is time we all remember that. We know his hands do good work. We are fearfully and wonderfully made for purpose!

Issues

You hypocrite, first take the plank out of your own eye, and then you will see clearly to remove the speck from your brother's eye.

—Matthew 7:5 NIV

Newspapers began as a way of passing pertinent information to the citizens of ancient Rome (Britannica Encyclopedia 2019). As civilizations grew, so did the need for newspapers and newspaper stands. My daughter once told me she knew a girl who had "so many issues she could open a newsstand." I thought that was hilarious. I laughed every time I thought about that analogy. Then I realized we could all open our own newsstand. When people see how we live, what would they be "reading"? Some may say the Bible, but even those people have issues.

Some of our newsstands would carry more tabloids than newspapers, but we all have issues. What would your stand look like? Would you have *Puzzle* magazines because people can't quite figure you out? Perhaps *Better Homes and Gardens* or maybe *Food TV*, in which case everything must look picture-perfect? How about *Teen* or maybe *Muscle* magazines, where people and bodies are idolized?

Most of our "issues" are based on past experiences and what we idolize. *People* magazine is popular, as is *National Enquirer*, because "inquiring minds want to know" so much about other people's lives and we are willing to accept what we read whether it's true or not. It's so easy to get caught up in the world of gossip and information that we sometimes forget to be mindful of our own lives. Take time to read what's in your newsstand. Is it a testimony you are willing to share?

Be Careful What You *Don't* Teach Your Children!

> Train up a child in the way he should go: and when he is old, he will not depart from it… He that soweth iniquity shall reap vanity: and the rod of his anger shall fail.
>
> —Proverbs 22:6, 8 KJV

Parents! Be it purposeful or not, we are our child's first and most important teacher. We teach them by what we do, what we say, and how we treat them and others. This is how values are passed from one generation to the next.

We teach our children how to eat by what we feed them. We teach them how to clean by how we keep our home. We teach them what to wear by the styles we ourselves admire. We teach them what's important by how we spend our time and money. Lessons aren't just by what we show them but also what we keep from them.

Both my husband and I are retired military members. Our children have been exposed to different cultures, thanks to our military service, and I believe that has allowed them to be more receptive to life changes. My husband and I raised three beautiful children who are now responsible, productive adults and are very much self-sufficient. They have each given their lives to Christ and are active in their home church. Did we do everything right? Not at all! But God…

The world has turned in such a way that common sense and courtesy are no longer being passed on. Be ye warned, if we don't teach our children the strategy of the enemy to our values, they will believe there is no enemy. If we as parents don't teach our children boundaries, they will believe there are none. If we as parents don't teach our children respect for others, they will believe theirs is the only thought that matters. If we don't teach our children there are consequences to our actions, they will continually do what they like without thought. They will be convinced that the rest of the world has been waiting for them to enter the stage so that it can revolve around them. What used to be common courtesy and common sense are no longer common. We should work on bringing common back.

Oh! The Beauty of It All

> Let the heavens rejoice, let the earth be glad; let the sea resound, and all that is in it. Let the fields be jubilant, and everything in them; let all the trees of the forest sing for joy.
>
> —Psalm 96:11–12 NIV

I HAVE A FOND MEMORY of driving from Farrell, Pennsylvania, to New York City in the late 1970s, a seven-to-nine-hour drive, depending on who's driving what. It was early summer, and I was going to visit family in New York before I moved to Germany where I was being stationed. It was such a beautiful, scenic drive. I had my music playing, with snacks and drinks within reach. Cruisin'. I remember thinking just how relaxing the drive was through Pennsylvania's wooded areas, regardless of how ragged the highway was. I actually think I got a little lost, but I didn't care. I had time. It was a beautiful day, not too hot, not too cool, but just right. But what I remember most vividly was coming out of a wooded area to suddenly an open area looking at trees, mountains, water, and the sunshine all at the same time. Birds were flying around and animals skittering about (somewhere I'm sure). Insects buzzed above the water. I was awestruck. That was the one moment in my life that I can truly say that nature took my breath away. At that moment, it was undeniable to me there is a God and he is worthy to be praised. A scene in the movie *Joe versus the Volcano* with Tom Hanks showed his character on a raft in the middle of the ocean. He was starving, dying of thirst, bone-weary, and without strength or hope. Suddenly, on the horizon, he saw the moon, how big and awesome it was. And he gained enough strength to stand and in awe lifted his hands, and as it sank below the horizon, he again lay down. I believe that to be a God-inspired moment.

On Purpose

Be anxious for nothing, but in everything by prayer and supplication, with thanksgiving, let your requests be made known to God; and the peace of God, which surpasses all understanding, will guard your hearts and minds through Christ Jesus.

—Philippians 4:6–7 NKJV

I HAVE A FRIEND WHO always has as her tagline "Have a blessed week on purpose" or something like that. She puts it at the end of her texts and emails and I think in her voice mail as well. I love that! Just typing the words makes me want to smile because it's a reminder of whose I am.

We all have good and bad days because we still live in a broken world. Being a Christian does not exclude us from experiencing pain or hurt or confusion or even terror. It just means we have been given a different way to deal with it. Scripture tells us to be anxious for nothing, but sometimes we are thrown off by situations or circumstances. So, when I get a text that ends with "Have a blessed week on purpose," I am reminded that I don't have to stress. God's got me.

There will be days when you are bombarded with hate, discouragement, fear, anger, and even sadness. But don't forget who you belong to. You belong to God, and he is on your side. When the going gets tough, the tough pray harder! Be intentional about your prayer because God is a prayer-answering God. He may not answer the way you think he should or even when, but he does answer.

Be intentional about your attitude because God is intentional about his attitude toward you. He has already shown how much he loves you by forgiving your sins. He refuses to turn his back on you no matter what you've done. His love abounds.

Be intentional about acknowledging your blessings. Start with the fact that you woke up today and understanding that not everyone did count that as a blessing. If you are healthy, count that as a blessing. Intentionally think of your many blessings. When you do that, you will be able to have a good day on purpose. Yup, that works!

Bitter Cup

> Saying, Father, if thou be willing, remove this cup from me: nevertheless not my will, but thine, be done.
>
> —Luke 22:42 KJV

When my son James was perhaps ten or eleven months old, he was busy playing on the floor, just crawling around followed by our five-year-old German shepherd, Jazei. Jazei was kind of following behind James. And I started noticing that she'd trot, then stop, and trot and then stop and James would crawl and then sit up and look back at Jazei as she stopped. Suddenly I realized Jazei was chewing something, something that James was dropping as he crawled. To my uttermost horror, I realized he was holding an open bottle of aspirin—uncoated, unwrapped, unadulterated, make-you-want-to-gag aspirin. I grabbed the aspirin off the floor, put Jazei outside (she had started throwing up), and grabbed James. I checked his mouth as I was dialing 911, and I could see some white powder on his lips, but there didn't seem to be any in his mouth.

Just to be on the safe side, I was told to take him to the emergency room. They drew blood, induced vomiting, and looked into every orifice of his poor little body to see if there were any ulcers or signs of poisoning. When all was said and done, I thank God they didn't find anything, but they still wanted to make sure they didn't miss anything. So they gave me a cup of charcoal and said he should drink as much as possible. My poor son was exhausted. All he wanted to do was sleep, but they wanted him to be alert, so I had to coax him awake. They gave me some 7 Up soda to add to the charcoal in hopes to make it more palatable. This drink was not just nasty but gritty as well. As I cuddled and whispered to him, he slowly drank most of the drink. After drinking the brew, he loudly burped and instantly went to sleep. He slept peacefully for more than two hours until the call of nature, helped by the charcoal, woke him. As we were leaving the hospital, I heard one of the techs whispering, "Did you see that kid drink that junk? What does that woman feed him?" I was too weary to say anything, but that they questioned what I fed my son because he drank that bitter drink hurt me, even angered me. I realized it wasn't that James was used to eating or drinking nasty things but that he trusted me. He trusted that if I was having him drink from this bitter cup, it would be for his good.

That's how we should trust God. Sometimes we may have to drink from a bitter cup. It may be that we must suffer loss of income, of our pride, of our health, or of a loved one, even at no fault of our own. God's allowing this not out of malice but out of love. Sometimes he allows us to go through some things that we may consider unnecessary or unfair. And yet, in the long run, we find it works out in our favor. Jesus so wanted the bitter "cup" to pass from him. It was not that Jesus was used to negative things happening. After all, he is a third of the Godhead. He was loved by many, had performed miracles, had walked through mobs untouched, and had a following of thousands. It was the circumstances in which he found himself, this place of betrayal and malice, that became his bitter cup. And yet... his obedience unto death allowed him to rise from the dead, fulfilling the prophecy and giving us the greatest gift of eternal life. "And He went a little farther and fell on His face and prayed, saying, 'O My Father, if it is possible, let this cup pass from Me, nevertheless, not as I will, but as Thou wilt'" (Matthew 26:39 KJV). Aren't you glad he trusted the Father?

Stand on It

> Not for that we have dominion over your faith, but are helpers of your joy: for by faith ye stand.
>
> —2 Corinthians 1:24 KJV

THE 13TH WARRIOR IS A dark little movie about Vikings, witchcraft, and battle. Right, wrong, or indifferent, I love this movie. It was this movie that made me realize how God teaches me things in the most "unusual" ways. The scene is in a Viking village being overrun by an enemy that they consider demon warriors. The "fire serpent" I believe is what they call them. The thirteenth warrior is not a Viking but an Arabian. He's not even a soldier but a diplomat who was sent to negotiate with the Vikings as punishment. He is much smaller in stature and less "barbaric" than the Vikings and has had to tolerate their ways of life. Nonetheless, when called upon, he fights fiercely beside them. At one point during this battle, the leader of the Vikings tosses him a huge wooden pole that has been sharpened at the top to look like a spear. It's approximately six inches in diameter and more than six feet long. You can tell he feels it is too long and bulky to use as a weapon, and he asks, "What do I do with this?" The leader sternly replies, "Stand on it!" as he leans the pole forward, places his foot on the bottom, and braces himself. As the enemy turns the corner, the poles pierce through the chest of their horses, throwing the riders to the ground where they are killed. Ultimately, the villagers end up winning the battle. At that moment, what jumped in my spirit was "Now that'll preach." I immediately understood how God's

Word works the same way. When we stand on his Word, the enemy, no matter the battle we are in, is thrown to the ground and put beneath our feet to be defeated. It became so plain to me I was almost giddy. Praise God for giving us his Word to stand on (Ephesians 6:11–14; 1 Thessalonians 3:8).

> Wherefore take unto you the whole armour of God, that ye may be able to withstand in the evil day, and having done all, to stand. (Ephesians 6:13 KJV)
>
> For now we live, if ye stand fast in the Lord. (1 Thessalonians 3:8 KJV)

Brace

> Therefore do not worry about tomorrow, for tomorrow will worry about itself. Each day has enough trouble of its own.
>
> —Matthew 6:34 NIV

MY FATHER'S BEST FRIEND WAS a big, burly guy he used to work with. They worked for the housing authority doing maintenance work in the public housing, or what we called the projects. His friend, Mr. Willie, liked playing jokes on people. Now, both men were strong. But like I said, Mr. Willie was a big guy, so when Daddy saw him struggling to carry a box down some stairs, he rushed up to meet him and braced himself to help carry this "heavy" load. He did not ask if he needed help; he just moved to help his friend. His muscles tightened in anticipation while his legs flexed to take on the extra weight. What my dad did not know was Mr. Willie was in one of his playful moods. When Daddy grabbed the box to take some of the load, he nearly fell down the stairs. His mind prepared his body for excessive weight only to find the box was empty. There was no excessive weight, yet Dad almost fell down a flight of stairs, bracing for something that was not there. He was worried about what was to come.

Looks, and thoughts, can be deceiving. Our minds calculate and cause our bodies to anticipate how we should handle the situation. The enemy will have you worrying about things that may never happen. That is why "faith" is so important. What we worry about is not always true, and having faith is not just about God fulfilling our wish list. Having faith is about trusting God in everything, especially those things we don't see or understand. We show faith by waiting for God to show us what to do next, how to handle a difficult situation or person, where to go, when to move, and what to pray for. There is only one thing we can be sure of in this life: God's intent for us to live a life more abundant. When your mind travels to what might happen, do not brace; trust.

You Have Need of a *Re-*

OFTENTIMES WE GO THROUGH LIFE as if we could never change our habits, or our trajectory in life. I'm here to tell you when there is that type of thinking, there is a need for a *re-*.

According to dictionary.com, "re-, a prefix, occurring originally in *loanwords* from *Latin*, used with the meaning 'again' or 'again and again' to indicate repetition, or with the meaning 'back' or 'backward' to indicate withdrawal or backward motion" (emphasis added).

Now, looking at the meaning, you may think *re-* is something bad, such as repetition or reject. But those things are not always bad.

Repetition

> Ask *and* keep on asking and it will be given to you; seek *and* keep on seeking and you will find; knock *and* keep on knocking and the door will be opened to you. For everyone who keeps on asking receives, and he who keeps on seeking finds, and to him who keeps on knocking, it will be opened. (Matthew 7:7–8 AMP, emphasis added)

THERE WILL BE TIMES IN your life when you find yourself seemingly stuck in a situation and you feel as if God didn't hear your prayers. That's not true. He hears everything you say. It's just not time for the answer yet. Sometimes God allows us to stay in a situation so that we can see for ourselves what is going on. If he takes us out of a situation too soon, we may never learn the lesson he has for us or appreciate the sacrifices needed to go to the next level. Remember *"everything works for the good of them that love the Lord."* So the next time you are frustrated with your situation, continue to pray about it. And as you pray, "ask" what lesson you need to learn, "seek" the direction he is leading you, and "knock" on the doors he leads you to. He will answer your questions, he will lead you where he wants you to go, and he will open the doors in due time.

Retreat

> But you, when you pray, go into your room, and when you shut your door, pray to your Father who is in the secret place; and your Father who sees in secret will reward you openly. (Matthew 6:6 NKJV)

Take solace again. Treat yourself to the presence, the love, the comfort, and the exclusivity of God. I believe things go much better when starting the day reading and praying God's Word. But sometimes, things don't go the way I want, and I get overwhelmed. When our peace is disturbed for whatever reason, our response should be to retreat, not react. Remember the enemy likes nothing better than to see us *re*acting badly, which damages our testimony. The enemy would also like us to believe that retreating is a weakness. To retreat is not a weakness but time to allow God to move on your behalf. It may be just for a moment that you would need to hold your tongue, quiet your spirit, and listen for direction from the Holy Spirit. Or it could be that you would need to step away to a quiet place, away from other people, and pray. Maybe for a few moments. Maybe for a few days. Just you and God alone in a secret place, a hiding place, that shuts out everyone, everything, every worry. And in that time, at that place, a transformation happens. Sometimes you may even be in the way of your own blessing. Move out of the way! The situation may not change, but your attitude will, and you can act as a follower of Christ should. Let him work on your behalf. Now that's a retreat.

Repeat

> But I tell you this—though he won't do it for friendship's sake, if you keep knocking long enough, he will get up and give you whatever you need because of your shameless persistence. And so I tell you, keep on asking, and you will receive what you ask for. Keep on seeking, and you will find. Keep on knocking, and the door will be opened to you. (Luke 11:8–9 NLT)

Muscles are built through the power of repetition. The more you work a muscle, the stronger it becomes. The same can be said of your relationship with God. Note that when you work a muscle, at first it may be painful. You may not even see results right away. But the more you work it, the stronger it becomes, and the more you will see results. So knock, pray, and see. In the interim, be patient. Patience is painful. But if you are willing to trust God and keep knowing, keep praying, and keep seeking, you will have your prayers answered. The more you go to God with your concerns, the stronger your spiritual relationship becomes, the more you see your need of him, and the more you will depend on him.

"Rejoice always, pray without ceasing, in everything give thanks. For this is the will of God in Christ Jesus for you" (1 Thessalonians 5:16–18 NKJV). Without ceasing. Continually. Repeat. Do it again and again and again.

Resign

> Look, the hour has come, and the Son of Man is delivered into the hands of sinners. Rise! Let us go! Here comes my betrayer! (Matthew 26:45 NIV)

Sometimes we don't know or understand why "we must go through," but God always has a plan to profit us, not destroy. Our resignation is not to be slaves to circumstance, but our resignation is knowing that God is in control. What we do, have, and are and where we go should be for his glory. And that happens when we resign ourselves to the fact that obedience to God is better than any sacrifice.

As I am writing this, I realize Jesus did all three of these things in Gethsemane. He repeatedly prayed for God to free him from this task. He retreated from his disciples so that he could speak with God alone. Then Jesus had resigned himself to what he knew needed to be done. In the verses prior, he had prayed that God "take this cup" from him. He didn't want to go forward in what he knew must come, but he accepted it and prepared his heart for it. And he resigned himself to it. And yet, we as humans consider these weaknesses or failures. But our strength, our help, comes from the Lord. "I lift up my eyes to the mountains—where does my help come from? My help comes from the Lord, the Maker of heaven and earth" (Psalm 121:1–2 NIV).

Remember/Return

> Yet I hold this against you: You have forsaken the love you had at first. Consider how far you have fallen! Repent and do the things you did at first. (Revelation 2:4–5 NIV)

Go back to doing what you did when you first were saved, like when you first fell in love. Be vulnerable in Christ. Be humble in spirit. Pour out your heart. Give God your all by loving and serving others. There is a saying that I heard once and have tried to live up to: "Don't be so heavenly bound that you are no earthly good." God didn't bless you for your sake but for the sake of others. What you have, share, be it finances, talent, compassion, or just a smile. I am ashamed to say as Christians, we can become quite callous. We tend to forget what God has delivered us from and turn our noses up at those that fall. You have turned away from your good works! Remember you, too, were once lost.

Can I Get a "Wow!"?

Habakkuk 2:2–3 (NLT) says, "This vision is for a future time. It describes the end, and it will be fulfilled. If it seems slow in coming, wait patiently, for it will surely take place. It will not be delayed."

When I was living in Germany, I met some wonderful godly women who encouraged me. As a group we started out calling ourselves WOG (Women of God). I don't know why we needed a name. But we began looking into other names, like WinGS (Women in God's Service) and W triple P (Women of Purpose, Prayer, and Praise), but then settled on WOW (Women of Worship). Why? Because we wanted to be God-centered, God-led, and God-wowed. There are so many times God has blown our minds all we could say was "Wow!" Haven't you ever felt that way? God has done something so awesome, so outlandish, so much a way out of no way that all you can do is fall to your knees and worship him? So inexplicable that all you can say is "Wow!" At least that's how I felt.

We only got to meet a couple of times. But in that time, we prayed for each other, encouraged each other, and pushed each other to do more. When we couldn't meet, we still texted each other, checked on each other, and generally stayed in touch. One of the activities we were to do was to create a vision board. Now I had heard of a vision board though never actually made one, but this assignment I took to heart. Habakkuk 2:2–3 (NLT) says, "Write my answer plainly on tablets, so that a runner can carry the correct message to others. This vision is for a future time. It describes the end, and it will be fulfilled. If it seems slow in coming, wait patiently, for it will surely take place. It will not be delayed." Believe it or not, this verse can so often be taken out of context, like now. But the intention is the same, to encourage. This was the beginning of God's answer to Habakkuk's complaint that he was allowing the enemies of Israel to get away with evil. Basically, God's reply was (paraphrased) "Write this down because I don't want to have to say it again. Let everyone know Israel will be all right." And he proceeded to explain how things were going to work out.

God gave me a couple of thoughts to share. Paraphrasing again, Romans 8:28 talks about how everything works out for the good. Psalm 34:4 says God will loose you of your fears! How awesome is that?

In this case, I am using this scripture to encourage you to make a vision board. On it should be all the things that God has promised and places he is leading you. Making a vision board is a must! And we must put our biggest, best dreams up on it. Do you believe you are to be an artist? A lawyer? A mother of five? Write it down. But write down only what God has shown you. One of the WOW asked a simple question, "What would you do if you were brave?" I answered that question by breaking it down into different categories. What would I do in ministry? For my family? For my health? For income? For a hobby? Praying about it helps. And I began to write… I put both long-term and short-term visions, and I was encouraged. Actually, that is how this book has come to fruition. Isn't God good!

Ponder Romans 8:28. Pray about it. Now think of your vision board. Can you see it? Is it what God has shown you? Is it God-sized? Do you feel overwhelmed or maybe even a little afraid? Do you feel it is too big for you to accomplish? You should. The vision should always be more than you are capable of if the vision is from God. Even your vision is a part of what will bring him glory. So make it big. Now read Psalm 34:4 again. What is it saying to you? Can I get a "Wow!"?

Growing Together in Christ

> Jesus replied: "Love the Lord your God with all your heart and with all your soul and with all your mind. This is the first and greatest commandment. And the second is like it: Love your neighbor as yourself."
>
> —Matthew 22:37–39 NIV

THE BASIS OF THIS SCRIPTURE is simple: relationship. You can't love anyone (or anything for that matter) without having a relationship.

"Growing together in Christ" was the 2018 tagline for a women's organization I belong to. I meditated on those four words, trying to see how we would grow together. I woke one morning at oh-dark-hundred to the fact that there are two ways to look at how we grow "together."

First, we as Christians grow *up* together like siblings might grow up together. They all have their own personality. And even when raised in the same house, under the same circumstances, they all grow in their own way, at their own pace. In families with more than one child, there is an order of birth. Even triplets have an oldest, middle, and youngest child. But that doesn't always determine the strength or maturity. Some grow strong and fast, others slow and steady, some straight and tall, while others not so much. But we are all growing up together under the watchful eye of a loving Father.

Then we grow together *in* Christ. We intermingle. Once you make your commitment to him, you are *in* Christ, just as plants are in soil. Being in the military, we live in a transient society. We are often moved from one city to another, sometimes even one country to another. As we move from one area to another, we often say we are transplanted. So, if we are transplanted, we are planted in a different garden each time and there are other plants in the same garden. Look at it as if where you live was a garden God has planted you in. So what happens when multiple plants are planted together? Do you know there are some plants that, when planted with other plants, can help to nourish other plants? God knows exactly who needs to be planted when and where. According to *Farmers' Almanac*, "It takes more than good soil, sun, and nutrients to ensure success in a garden. Time-honored gardening wisdom says that certain plants, when grown together, improve each other's health and yields. For instance, some plants attract beneficial insects that help to protect a companion, while other plants (particularly herbs) act as repellents."[1] As Christ continues to anoint, appoint, and nourish each of us, our roots become intertwined. We become interdependent. We need to recognize that we are set apart for a purpose, so we must encourage each other to stay in Christ. Receive grace and give grace. Love God, and love God's people.

Silent Night

> But ask now the beasts, and they shall teach thee; and the fowls of the air, and they shall tell thee: Or speak to the earth, and it shall teach thee: and the fishes of the sea shall declare unto thee... In whose hand is the soul of every living thing, and the breath of all mankind?
>
> —Job 12:7–8, 10 KJV

I believe "Silent Night" is one of the most beautiful and precious songs ever written. It touches my heart no matter what mood I may be in. Have you ever seen the movie *Last Holiday* with Queen Latifah? There is a scene where she walks into the lobby of this fabulous hotel, she looks up at the wonderfully ornate ceiling, and says, "Don't that just make you want to cry?" That is how I feel about "Silent Night." It is such a beautiful song. No matter who sings it, with or without music, solo or full choir, it is just beautiful! The song was written in Austria by a priest by the name of Joseph Mohr in 1816.[2] It is believed he wrote it after an evening walk on a bright and silent night.

In my mind, I imagine being a shepherd the night Christ was born. Just before the angels showed up, I imagine the sheep would suddenly stop bleating. There would be no birds chirping, no canine howling, no insects skittering. Even the winds would stop blowing. Total silence. But instead of becoming anxious, there would be a calm, a peace beyond all understanding, that would come over all of nature. All creation would be silent with anticipation and awe, almost as if in prayer. Why? Because all things created would recognize the "Creator" was entering the world. That song personifies what nature knew. It was a "holy night." I can imagine so clearly the stillness, the silence, the peace. I can imagine a single voice breaking the silence to sing that song soft as a lullaby. Then soon after the angels would announce his arrival to us in the fields. I know I have quite an imagination, but it works.

So, before the celebrations, the parties, the great galas, before the angelic voices, the presentations, and the presents, be silent. Be in awe of the thought that over two thousand years ago, the Creator, the King of kings, the Prince of peace, Emmanuel, God, poured himself into an earthly vessel, in the humblest of beginnings just for the sole purpose of relating to you and me. That is what "Silent Night" means to me.

Notes

[1] https://www.almanac.com/content/companion-planting-guide
[2] https://www.wrti.org/post/story-behind-beloved-christmas-carol-silent-night
[3] YouVersion Bible App + audio

About the Author

THE YOUNGEST OF FOUR CHILDREN, Mrs. Flack was born in New York and raised in Pennsylvania where she accepted Christ as a teenager. After graduating high school, she joined the United States Air Force where she met her husband. They have three adult children, each serving God in their own way. She has voluntarily served in the military chapel service or local church, wherever they lived, including Kansas, Texas, California, Okinawa, Germany, and Arizona. She has been a part of the praise team, choir, public relations, and writers' group and has been a Bible study facilitator and a women's group leader. She has retired from the military and is currently living in Arizona with her husband.

Printed in the USA
CPSIA information can be obtained
at www.ICGtesting.com
LVHW100756250923
759082LV00001B/368